STUFF EVERY

WINE SNOB

SHOULD KNOW

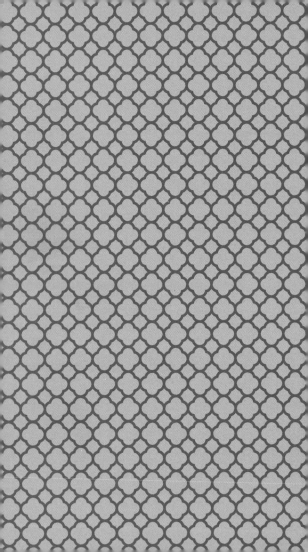

STUFF EVERY

WINE
SNOB

SHOULD KNOW

QUIRK BOOKS
PHILADELPHIA

Library of Congress Cataloging in Publication Number: 2017941580

ISBN: 978-1-68369-019-1

Printed in China

Cover design by Andie Reid
Typeset in Goudy and Akzidenz-Grotesk

Production management by John J. McGurk

Quirk Books
215 Church Street
Philadelphia, PA 19106
quirkbooks.com

10 9 8 7 6 5

IN MEMORY OF

MY MOTHER,

ROBERTA MONOSOFF

LIVING YOUR WINE SNOB LIFE

Introduction

I fell in love with wine when I was a student at the Culinary Institute of America. It was the first subject I was addicted to knowing everything about. What a revelation that a simple glass of wine was so much more: a time, a place, a person, a piece of ground, a war, history, geology, chemistry, biology, botany, enology . . . and the list goes on!

In the beginning, I loved studying wine, but I didn't like drinking it much. Given that, until then, my wine experience was Manischewitz on Passover, most likely from last year's bottle still sitting on the lazy Susan, this is hardly surprising. (I often showed off to my friends by sneaking one of the adult plastic cups of wine at the synagogue and pouring it into a kids' cup. I thought I was getting away with the crime of the century!)

So it took me a while to get used to the taste and structure of classic wines. However, as my culinary world widened, my palate developed. Today, the mouth-numbing tannins of a great Barolo and the mouth-puckering tartness of beautiful Champagne are some of my very favorite things in this world.

But what really keeps me in love is the magic in wine: how it brings people together to share a common experience. Wine can be studied, of course, but it can also be a major contributor to our emotions, memories, social interactions, and connections. Just the name of a variety or the sight of a bottle can be enough to transport you to a specific time and place or call to mind a special person or event.

Most of all, wine is an avenue to adventure and a lifetime of learning. I hope this book provides some inspiration for fun, exploration, and experimentation. We will take a peek into the immense world of wine with a bit of history, as well as information on how different styles are made, major growing regions, grape varieties, how to taste wine, and how to pair wine with food. Plus some pro tips from a master sommelier (*moi*) on how to survive at restaurants that have encyclopedic wine lists.

Remember: it's just wine—so let's have some fun. *Santé!*

WINE
BASICS

Highlights from Wine History

As one of the world's oldest beverages, wine has quite the historical pedigree. Here are some landmark dates in the evolution of our favorite drink.

Ca. 7000 BCE: First evidence of wine production: Chinese pottery shards later discovered in Henan province show residue of wine made from both grapes and rice.

Ca. 4100 BCE: Approximate date of first known winery, located in the Areni-1 cave in Armenia.

Ca. 3000 BCE: Royal wine making begins in Egypt, with grapes likely crushed by foot.

Ca. 300 BCE: Ancient Greek writer Theophrastus describes contemporary wine-making practices, including complex pairings of soil types with grape varieties and methods for minimizing yields (and thereby concentrating flavor).

121 BCE: Year of the so-called Opimian vintage of Roman wine, prized into the next century for its supreme quality.

71 CE: The first vineyards are planted in Bordeaux by Romans, possibly from cuttings from the Rioja region of Spain.

77 CE: Pliny the Elder publishes his *Naturalis Historia*, the text from which the phrase *in vino veritas* (in wine, there is truth) is adapted.

79 CE: Mount Vesuvius erupts, destroying the city of Pompeii and interrupting trade, causing wine to become scarce and prices for it to soar.

Ca. 200 CE: Romans begin to use the screw press to crush grapes.

1152 CE: The marriage of Henry II of England and Eleanor of Aquitaine causes a spike in the cost of Bordeaux wines.

1435: Count John IV of Katzenelnbogen plants the first riesling grapes near Frankfurt, Germany.

1524: Vineyards are established in Mexico by Spanish settlers.

1630: Sir Kenelm Digby begins to manufacture glass wine bottles sturdy and strong enough for general use.

1685: Simon van der Stel, governor of the Dutch Cape Colony in the Cape of Good Hope, South Africa, founds what is now Groot Constantia, the country's oldest winery.

1718: Benedictine monk Dom Pérignon's winemaking rules are published.

1788: Wine cuttings are brought to New South Wales, Australia (then a penal colony), from South Africa.

1798: First Vineyard, America's first commercial winery, is established by John DuFour in Nicholasville, Kentucky.

1863: The "great French wine blight," which would destroy 40 percent of French vineyards by the mid-1870s, begins.

1851: Chilean industrialist Silvestre Ochagavia imports cuttings of French vines to cultivate in his own country.

1920: Prohibition, the nationwide ban on alcohol in the United States, takes effect until 1933; during this period, more than 2,000 American wineries are shuttered.

1935: France's *Comité national des appellations d'origine* is created to standardize and regulate the naming of wines for specific regions.

1935: Australian Thomas Angove invents a "cask wine" (aka boxed wine) container consisting of a polyethylene bladder housed in a corrugated cardboard box.

1976: The so-called Judgment of Paris competition is held, at which French wine judges declare California-made cabernet sauvignon and chardonnay superior to those made in France.

1980s: New Zealand sauvignon blanc puts the country on the map as a producer of high-quality wines.

Terms Every Wine Snob Should Know

Need to brush up on your oenophile* speak? Here are the terms you'll need to know.

Acidity: One of the five taste sensations. Acidity in wine activates the salivary glands and creates a sour or tart sensation and enlivening, refreshing, and crisp quality.

Aeration: Exposing wine to oxygen to release aromas and flavors (aka letting the wine breathe)

Alcohol: Ethanol (ethyl alcohol); the product of fermentation of sugars by yeast

Appellation: A delimited wine-producing region, i.e., a place with a protected name

Astringent: A tasting term noting the harsh, bitter, and drying sensations in the mouth caused by high levels of tannin

---

*See page 19.

Balance: The result of all the elements of a wine, such as acids, sugars, tannins, alcohol, and flavor, coming together harmoniously

Barrel: A container made of oak that is used for fermenting and aging wine

Bitter: A taste sensation caused by the tannins in grapes

Blend: A wine made from more than one grape varietal

Blind tasting: Evaluating wine without knowledge of the grape, country of origin, or vintage year

Body: The sensation or perception of the weight of wine on the palate; can be described as light, medium, or full

Claret: The British name for the red wines of Bordeaux, France

Complex: A tasting term used to describe a wine that exhibits many aromas and flavors

Corked/corky: A term for wine that has a musty, moldy, cardboard or chlorine smell or flavor caused by a defective cork

Cuvée: A blend or batch of wine

Decanter: A carafe used to aerate wine or separate older wine from deposited sediment

Dry: A tasting term used to describe wine with little or no residual sugar; the opposite of sweet (see page 50)

Earthy: A tasting term used to describe wine with an aroma or flavor of soil

Fermentation: The conversion of grape sugars to alcohol by the action of yeast

Finish: The length of time a wine's flavor lingers on the palate; the longer and more harmonious the finish, the higher the quality of the wine

Fruity: Imparting aromas and flavors of fresh fruit

Hot: A word used to describe wine that is noticeably high in alcohol

Mature: A term indicating that a wine is ready to drink

Mouthfeel: How a wine feels on the palate, such as rough, smooth, velvety, or furry

New world: Non-European wine-producing regions, such as North America, South America, South Africa, Australia, and New Zealand

Nose: A tasting term describing the smell of a wine; also called *aroma* or *bouquet*

Oak/oaky: Tasting term denoting smells and flavors of vanilla, baking spices (like cinnamon, clove, and nutmeg), coconut, mocha, or dill; a quality of wine that has been fermented or aged in oak barrels (see page 57)

Oenophile: A fancy word for "wine snob," from the Greek *oinos* (wine) and *philos* (love)

Old world: The winemaking regions of Europe: France, Italy, Germany, et al.

Plonk: A derogatory name for cheap wine

Reserve: A term often seen on U.S. wine labels that is not legally defined and whose meaning differs among producers who use it

Sediment: Compounds in wine that have settled over time and formed a layer at the bottom of the bottle. Young wines made from highly pigmented grape varieties can also throw sediment as well.

Sommelier: A wine steward or the person in charge of the wine list or beverage program at a restaurant

Spicy: A tasting term used for odors and flavors reminiscent of black pepper, bay leaf, curry powder, baking spices, oregano, rosemary, thyme, saffron, or paprika

Sweet: Describes a wine with perceptible sugar content (see page 50)

Tannins: Natural compounds in grape skins, seeds, and stems that impart a bitter flavor in wine and act as preservatives

Tartrates: Crystals appearing on the cork or at the bottom of a bottle of wine that separate from the liquid during aging; the harmless result of the natural tartaric acid in grapes and potassium in wine

Terroir: The French concept of a wine showing a "sense of place" (see page 28)

Vineyard: The land used to grow grapevines

Vinification: The art of wine making

Vintage: The calendar year in which grapes are harvested for wine

Viticulture: The art of grape growing

Vitis vinifera: A European species of grapevine that produces the majority of the world's quality wine

Winery: A company or establishment that produces wine; may, but does not always, grow its own grapes

Yeast: A microorganism that converts grape sugars into alcohol

Yield: The productivity of a vineyard or vine

TO CAPITALIZE OR NOT?

If you're a detail-oriented wine snob, you may notice that sometimes varieties are capitalized and other times they are not. What's the deal? If a wine (or the grape for which it is named) takes its name from a place *and is from that place*, the name of the wine should be capitalized. Some champagne is grown in California so it is not capitalized; the stuff that hails from Champagne, France, gets an uppercase C. (For more on this, see page 66.) Meanwhile, lots of wine and grape names have nothing to do with a place name—nebbiolo's name comes from the Italian word for "fog," and pinot noir comes partly from the French for "pine cone," a reference to the shape of the grape's bunches. Laws that govern the use of a particular name, such as for brandy made in the region of Cognac, can also help you decide whether to capitalize or lowercase. In the case of wines whose name is a variant of their places of origin (e.g., sherry from Jerez, Spain), no capitalization is needed.

The Life Cycle of a Grapevine

The quality of grapes is the single factor that most directly affects the quality of the wine. Although technically both nature and nurture influence a wine's quality, as the old adage goes, "great wine is made in the vineyard." You simply cannot make quality wine without high-quality fruit. (Of course, a subpar winemaker can turn perfect grapes into plonk, but not even a seasoned expert can make good wine from low-quality grapes.)

Grapevines are a perennial plant, meaning they bloom over spring and summer, die back during fall and winter, and return on their own the following spring. Without the human influence of a vineyard manager, who oversees pruning and training, a grapevine will naturally grow unfettered into crazy-haired tendrils instead of producing quality fruit. During the first few years of a vine's life, energy is spent building up nutrient stores, a strong trunk, and a solid root system. By the third year or so, the vine is ready to produce quality fruit for wine making. Let's look at a year in the life of a vine and at how each season impacts the growth of the grape clusters.

SPRING

- **Bud break:** In April or May, sap rises and small shoots and leaves begin to break through buds left from the winter pruning (more on that later). The buds are extremely vulnerable to frost during this time. The leaves of the vine continue to grow and small green clusters called embryo bunches form on the shoots.

- **Flowering:** The little embryo bunches bloom into small flowers for about 10 days. The flowers are highly susceptible to damage caused by wind (which can blow the little flowers off the bunch), cold, and frost.

- **Fertilization and fruit set:** Grapevines are self-pollinating. Fruit set refers to the stage when successfully pollinated embryo bunches grow into grape clusters; each grape is the product of individual fertilization.

SUMMER/EARLY FALL

- **Berry growth/*véraison*:** In June and July, young clusters of fruit begin to appear and grow. At this stage the berries are hard, high in acidity, and low in sugar. In August, *véraison* (the viticultural term for the onset of ripening) begins and the grapes start to ripen fully, as sugars move from the leaves of the plant to the fruit. Now the grapes soften and change color, turning from green to red (for red grapes) or yellowish green (for white grapes). Sugar rises further and acidity decreases. Cane ripening occurs along with *véraison*, during which the stems on each shoot begin to lignify (harden), accumulating carbohydrates to sustain the plant through the winter.

- **Harvest:** Once the grapes have achieved an ideal balance of sugar and acid, they are ready for harvest (*vendange*). This can occur as early as August and as late as the beginning of November, depending on the grape variety and the climate of the wine region. In that short, sweet-spot window of time, vineyard workers toil 24/7 to harvest the grapes.

LATE FALL AND WINTER

- **Slowing down:** Like most plants, vines lose their leaves in fall: first, the vine stops producing carbohydrates from the chlorophyll, then the leaves change from green to yellow, and finally the leaves drop from the vine around the first frost. For late-harvest wines, grapes are left on the vine well into the fall and, in the case of ice wine, even into the snowy winter. The grapes raisinate (dry out) or freeze and are later pressed to make a very sweet dessert wine.

- **Pruning and maintenance:** In winter, vines enter a period of dormancy. Trimming and pruning help to maintain them through the cold months until the beginning of the next year's cycle.

How the Vineyard Affects the Wine

Cultivating grapes requires a myriad of decisions from vineyard growers and winemakers and is influenced by many factors. Many wineries, especially in the new world (or the non-European countries of the wine-making world), make many different styles of wine to appeal to a wide market, while in the old world (or the traditional European wine-making countries), the grape varieties that may be grown and the style of wine made are dictated by strict wine law. Here are a few of the factors at the vineyard level that affect wine before it even hits your glass.

CLIMATE

After the characteristics and flavors of certain grape varieties, climate has the most influence on style and flavor. In cooler climates, grapes ripen less in the vineyard, so they contain less sugar and more acidity, producing tarter, leaner wines that often have a subtle fruit character. Conversely, in warmer climates, grapes ripen more in the vineyard, giving them higher sugar levels, which can translate into higher alcohol content and produce fruitier wine.

TERROIR

You may have heard this word bandied about in wine circles. Originally a French term, *terroir* does not have a direct English translation, but it refers to a sense of place: the idea that a wine region, vineyard, or selection of vines can impart a unique set of characteristics from the microclimate, soil, topography, and weather that makes wine from that region taste distinctly different from others. The idea is that a wine is not just about grapes, but a holistic combination of the vine and its environment. However, terroir is a hotly debated topic: there is no consensus on *how* those factors translate into the wine, but there is also no doubt that certain wines show a set of unique and identifiable characteristics that come from a combination of the above factors. The concept of terroir forms the basis of the French appellation system, or the way the French label their wines and regulate and protect place names. (This is one reason most French—and really most European—wines are named for the place they come from.)

OLD WORLD VS. NEW WORLD

The wide world of wine is often divided into these two categories. The old world wines hail from Europe, and wines from North America, South

America, South Africa, Australia, and New Zealand are considered new world. Generally the old world produces earthier wines while the new world produces wines that are more fruit-driven, although exceptions exist and characteristics can vary by climate and region (and even winery!).

GRAPES

Although well more than a thousand grape varieties are grown for commercial wine production across the globe, not all grapes can be grown everywhere. Many grow best in specific climates and soil types. For instance, riesling, nebbiolo, and pinot noir are pretty fussy grape varieties that thrive only in very specific conditions. Others, like chardonnay, merlot, and even cabernet sauvignon, are more versatile and can be (and are) grown in many climates. Many of the most beloved wines are made from grapes that were born and bred in France and are now planted across the globe. Although varieties of grapes present differently—just like various breeds of dogs and cats look different—the vast majority of the wine we drink is from the species *Vitis vinifera*. Cabernet sauvignon, merlot, riesling, chardonnay, and pinot noir are all examples of *Vitis vinifera*.

HARVESTING TIMING

Exactly when—meaning the specific day and in some cases even the hour—the grapes should be picked and brought to the winery is crucial. The sweet spot depends on the grape variety, the region, the climate where the wine will be made, and the style of wine being produced. At the heart of the decision is the physiology of the grapes: the goal is to find balance in the pulp between the fruit's natural acids and the sugar produced during the growing season and, sometimes, to hit the perfect ripeness of the grape seeds and skins (particularly important if harvesting red grapes). Timing is everything, and weather changes influence when to pick. Intense rain will fill the grapes with water and dilute that precious balance. A heat wave would cause the grapes to ripen very quickly, spiking the sugar level and dropping the balancing acidity.

Also, grapes do not continue to ripen once picked. Harvesting grapes on the early side produces wines with elevated acidity and lower alcohol (due to less sugar ripeness). In grapes that are picked later, that balance flips—the grapes are full of sugar and low in acidity, producing wines that are very ripe in flavor but may need an acid adjustment in the winery; winemakers can regain that balance and make the wine drinkable by adding tartaric, malic, or citric acid. Without proper acidity, the wine will feel flabby and flat in the mouth.

HARVESTING METHOD

The quality of the wine is also influenced by whether the grapes are harvested by hand or by machine and how they are brought to the winery. When harvested by hand, the best bunches are picked clean of bugs and excess leaves and laid into small baskets to prevent premature bruising or crushing, both of which can lead to fermentation and oxidation—not ideal for quality wine making! Furthermore, some vineyards are planted on incredibly steep slopes, making hand harvesting the only choice. Many sweet wines are made from hand-picked grapes to ensure that only the perfect grapes for the style of wine are used.

Machine harvesting is quick and efficient, but does not differentiate good grapes from bad, which makes sorting a necessity. This is not to say this method is inferior—some of the top wine estates in the world harvest by machine. During sorting, the grapes move along a conveyor belt and are inspected for quality; undesirable grapes and detritus from the vineyard are removed. And even with the best grapes, preventing oxidation is the name of the game. The quicker the grapes get to the winery, the greater the potential for quality wine.

From Grape to Glass: How Wine Is Made

In the simplest scientific terms, wine is the juice of grapes whose natural sugars have been fermented into alcohol by the presence of yeast.

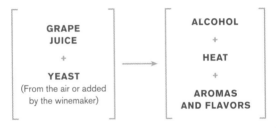

The chemical reaction is simple, yet the myriad differences in aroma and flavor created through fermentation is mind-boggling. Many factors come into play, such as how and where the grapes were grown, decisions made by the winemakers, and, of course, Mother Nature. Ultimately, wine is oh so much more than a chemical reaction: in each glass, we get a taste of history and tradition, a sense of place, and insight into the personality of the winemaker.

So how does a wine go from grapes growing on a vine to a drink with beautiful aromas and flavors such as strawberry, raspberry, black tea, ginger, vanilla, wet stone, and leather?

Most wine making begins the same way: the grapes are transported from the vineyard to the winery, sorted for quality, and cleaned of detritus. Next, the grapes are crushed and destemmed—the individual winemaker decides whether the grapes are taken off the stem before crushing or crushed as whole bunches. Then the process varies depending on the type of wine being made. Here's a breakdown of each style.

WHITE WINES

Although white grapes are associated with white wine, grapes of any color can be used because the pulp of most grapes is clear. So you can make white wine from any red grape variety—you just need to remove the skins (where the color is).

1. Pressing: The grapes are pressed to release their juice. The skins and other solids may be discarded immediately or left to hang out with the juice for a few hours, which allows for aromatic compounds from the solids to be extracted.

2. Fermentation: The sugars in the juice are fermented by the addition of yeasts, creating alco-

hol, heat, and carbon dioxide (CO_2). For white wines, fermentation is slow and done at cooler temperatures to preserve freshness and vibrancy of the grape variety. Fermentation takes two weeks or more, depending on grape variety and climate, to reach the desired level of dryness. Remember: the yeasts are eating all the natural grape sugars in the wine, so the more sugars they eat, the drier the wine will be.

3. Aging . . . sometimes: Depending on the wine style being made, the winemaker will decide if the wine should be aged and how. Most light, aromatic white wines are not aged and are bottled shortly after fermentation. Other, more robust whites are aged in oak barrels, imparting toasty, vanilla, and spice flavors. How long wines are aged depends on winemaker, but generally white wines are aged for less time than reds.

RED WINES

When making red wine, pressing occurs after fermentation; the pigment in those grape skins needs to sit with the grape juice to give it a rich red color. Each grape variety gives a different hue, ranging from ruby to garnet to purple.

1. Maceration/skin contact: The grapes are crushed, and the juice, skins, and seeds sit together for days, weeks, or even months. For red wine, the skins are retained for color as well as greater tannin and flavor.

2. Fermentation: The sugars in the juice are fermented by the action of yeasts into alcohol, heat, and carbon dioxide (CO_2). Fermentation of red wine is done more quickly (one to three weeks) and at much warmer temperatures than white wine, to help retain color and flavor from the grape skins. New aromas and flavors also emerge as a result of the greater number of chemical reactions that occur in a warm fermentation.

3. Pressing: Now the red grapes are pressed, separating the liquid from the skins and other solids.

4. Aging . . . sometimes: Just as with white wine, a winemaker can decide whether a red wine will be aged and, if so, how. The choice invariably depends on the style of wine being made, but in many wine regions, especially in the old world, minimum amounts of aging in oak, in bottles, or both are encoded in law. For instance, a top Napa cabernet could be aged in barrels for eighteen

months to two years, but a basic pinot noir, which may not benefit from long aging, could spend a few months or even a few weeks in the barrel.

ROSÉ

Making rosé begins like red-wine making and ends like white-wine making. (In fact, there are two ways of making rosé: one is by mixing white wine with red wine to create pink wine. This is rarely done, however, and not legal for many rosés aside from the high-profile and expensive rosé Champagne bottlings. The other is a more standard wine-making process.)

1. Maceration/skin contact: If we want pink wine, we have to keep those skins in contact with the juice, but only for a short time, just a few hours (up to a day), depending on the desired color.

2. Pressing: The skins and other solids are discarded, since the wine has all the color it needs.

3. Alcohol fermentation: Similar to white wines, rosé fermentation is slow (two weeks or more) and done at cooler temperatures to preserve the freshness and vibrancy of the grape variety.

4. Aging . . . rarely: To preserve the pretty, youthful fruit character of rosé, aging in oak is rare.

Know Your Grapes: White

As you know, white wine can be made from red grapes as well as from white (see page 33). However, white grapes are still an essential part of wine making! Here is a rundown of classic grapes and up-and-comers and the top regions that make wine from them.

THE CLASSICS

CHARDONNAY

Chardonnay is an incredibly versatile variety that grows well in many conditions. In cool climates like Chablis, France, the wine shows tarter fruit flavors like lemon and green apple and has more intense, delicious minerality. In other parts of Burgundy, like Meursault, Chassagne, and Puligny-Montrachet, the wines have riper fruit flavors, like those of yellow apples and pears. (These are often aged in new French oak, which gives scents of vanilla, toast, and spice.) Chardonnay takes well to aging in new oak, which is done most prominently in the new world, yielding warm-climate wines that show more intense ripe fruit character and loads of vanilla bean, toast, butterscotch, cinnamon, and clove. A buttery or buttered popcorn flavor is often associated with some chardonnays made in California.

SAUVIGNON BLANC

Sauvignon blanc grown in the cooler climates of the Loire Valley produces wines that are clean, crisp, and lean. In order to preserve the grape's inherent mineral, lime citrus, grassy character, these wines are not aged in new oak. In Bordeaux, sauvignon blanc is richer and is blended with sémillon, which gives the wine a rich, almost waxy texture; the best examples are oak aged. In the new world, especially California, sauvignon blanc may be either oak aged, and then often sold under the moniker fumé blanc, for the smoky (*fumé*) character the oak gives the wine, or aged without oak, yielding a crispy and dry wine with riper citrus and tree fruit character. New Zealand sauvignon blanc is distinctive for this varietal, with intense aromas of lime, grapefruit, passion fruit, jalapeño pepper, and lemongrass.

RIESLING

This grape prefers cooler climates, is rarely blended, and can be fermented into many different styles that run the gamut from bone dry to lusciously sweet. The popular belief that all rieslings are sweet simply is not true. In southwestern Germany near the borders of France and Luxembourg, along the banks of the many prominent rivers such as the Rhine and Mosel, are some of the most precipitous vineyards, which garner warmth from light reflected off the rivers that helps the grapes ripen in the region's cool climate. These vineyards are most known for delicious off-dry styles, and more and more dry wines are coming to our shores. Alsace, France, produces dry and off-dry styles, and Austria and South Australia are known for drier styles. In the United States, both Washington state and the Finger Lakes of New York make delicious, high-quality riesling.

PINOT GRIS/PINOT GRIGIO

Pinot gris and pinot grigio are two names (the first French, the second Italian) for the same grape variety, which often indicate individual styles. Pinot gris from Alsace, France, produces wines that are ripe and rich due to the area's climate. Some Alsatian pinot gris are slightly off-dry. Pinot grigio from northeastern Italy is crisp, dry, minerally, and unoaked. In Oregon, styles vary depending on the producer.

THE UP-AND-COMERS

CHENIN BLANC
The middle section of France's Loire Valley is chenin blanc country. This grape produces every conceivable style of wine, from sparkling to dry, off-dry, and sweet. Examples include Vouvray, Montlouis, bone-dry Savennières, and dessert wine such as Coteaux du Layon. South Africa is one of the only other wine regions that specializes in chenin blanc, producing both oaked and unoaked styles.

VIOGNIER
This grape is naturally very floral in character and produces a rich, almost voluptuous style of white wine. The top areas of production are Condrieu, in the northern Rhône Valley of France, and many parts of California. New oak is being used less with these wines than in the past to let the unique character shine through.

GRÜNER VELTLINER
The hallmark grape variety of Austria, and an extremely versatile one at that! The grape yields crisp, dry, unoaked wines with prominent lime, floral, and savory herb notes.

ALBARIÑO

Rías Baixas, the northwestern corner of Spain bordering the Atlantic, specializes in this aromatic white variety. It makes a pretty and unoaked wine with aromas and flavors of peaches, apricot, minerals, and a little hint of the sea air from the nearby ocean.

GEWÜRZTRAMINER

Alsace, France, is the world's largest producer of this love-it-or-hate-it variety. The full-bodied wines from this grape have one-of-a-kind intense aromas of lychee and roses. Wines can be dry or off-dry depending on the producer, and they're delicious with spicy food and intensely flavored cheeses.

Know Your Grapes: Red

Vines that produce red grapes can be planted in many different regions but thrive in moderate to warm climates, where they can ripen properly. (Notice that in warmer climates, the majority of grape varieties grown are red, and in cooler climates, mainly white grapes are grown.) Red grapes need a bit longer to ripen, to ensure that the skins and seeds are flavorful and not overly bitter. Each of the following varieties is unique in the size of its berries and clusters and in the amount of color in the skins, which directly affects the color of the wine. (I always say never judge a wine by its color. Some of the lightest-colored wines pack the biggest punch.)

THE CLASSICS

PINOT NOIR

Also known as "the diva," this is a picky vine that is difficult to grow well. It originates in Burgundy, France, home to some of the priciest wines (and some of the most expensive real estate!) on the planet. Earthy in flavor, light in color, and with modest amounts of tannins, the wines made from this grape are extremely food friendly and, in the hands of the right winemaker, packed with flavor. California's Sonoma Coast and the Santa Rita Hills in Santa Barbara and some regions of Oregon yield top-notch pinot noir wines with richness and soft, elegant tannins.

CABERNET SAUVIGNON

This is one of the most-planted quality grape varieties on the planet because it can thrive in a wide range of climates, from Canada to Australia. The progeny of cabernet franc and sauvignon blanc, this grape is also of French origin, and it is grown primarily in Bordeaux, France; California and Washington state in the U.S.; and Australia. It has aromas and flavors of blackberry, black plum, and cassis, plus a signature herbal and bell pepper note. Most often blended with cabernet franc and merlot (another member of its family), cabernet sauvignon may also be oak aged to add a vanilla and spice character. These wines can be incredibly bold and full flavored, with elevated levels of tannin.

MERLOT

Like cabernet sauvignon, merlot is widely planted thanks to its ability to produce quality wines in many climates. Flavors and aromas are similar to cabernet sauvignon, but with a little more red-fruit character, dark chocolate, and the signature bell pepper. Merlot is often oak aged, and primary growing areas include Bordeaux, France; and California and Washington state in the U.S.

SYRAH/SHIRAZ

From Côte-Rôtie and Hermitage in the Rhône Valley of France to Australia, this grape is a world traveler. Syrah is the French name for this varietal, and Shiraz is how it's known in new world growing areas such as Australia, South Africa, and the U.S. (The discrepancy may be the result of a mispronunciation or botched transcription of the name when the grape first came to Australia in the 1830s.) In the old world, or in cooler climates, Syrah produces wines with complex, smoky bacon aromas and flavors of herbes de Provence, black pepper, and olives. In the new world, or in warm climates, that same black olive and black pepper character emerges, with a backdrop of intense and often jammy fruit such as dried blackberry, blueberry, and fig. Top areas of production are France, Washington state, and Australia.

THE UP-AND-COMERS

GAMAY

Mainly found in the Beaujolais region of France, this cool-climate grape variety produces wines that are lighter in color, similar to pinot noir, and soft in tannins, often with a candied-fruit character. Given its versatility in food pairings, it's a real unsung (or undersung) hero.

MALBEC

This grape variety from southwest France was brought to Argentina in the 1800s. In the last decade or so, Argentine malbec has taken on a life of its own and has become an incredibly popular wine choice. The love for malbec stems from its rich black fruit character, supple soft tannins, and excellent value.

ZINFANDEL

This variety may share DNA with an obscure European grape, but its roots are firmly planted in California. We can thank the production and popularity of sweet pink white zinfandel for keeping this grape variety around. The old vines from which it's grown—some of which were planted more than fifty years ago!—produce a delicious, intense, ripe, fruit-driven style that is often aged in oak, giving the wine a spicy, toasty character.

GRENACHE
Originally from Spain, where it's often called garnacha, this grape made its way up to France's southern Rhône Valley and has become the primary grape in the quaffable Côtes du Rhône and the stately Gigondas and Châteauneuf-du-Pape. Grenache loves warm climates and produces wines with aromas of strawberry, cured meat, leather, mushrooms, and herbs. Australian grenache from the Barossa Valley is a great new world example.

NEBBIOLO
Hailing from Piedmont, Italy, nebbiolo is the grape variety used to make Barolo and Barbaresco. Its very light color belies its incredible aromatics of dried roses, cherries, raspberry, and leather. The wine has high tannin and high acidity, which are easily placated with the rich local cuisine (think: pasta with cream sauces, game meats, and white truffle).

SANGIOVESE
Known as the "king of Tuscany," sangiovese is the primary grape variety of classic wines like Chianti Classico, Brunello di Montalcino, and Vino Nobile di

Montepulciano. The wines are aromatic, with cherry, plum, and pomegranate; savory herbs like oregano and sage; and a structured, tannin-rich backbone.

TEMPRANILLO

This is the main grape in the wines of many of Spain's top wine regions like Rioja and Ribera del Duero. Depending on the producer and the region, the resulting wines can be complex, even rustic, with a ripe dried-fruit character and many earthy, leathery, tobacco notes.

CABERNET FRANC

From the Loire Valley of France, this grape makes one-of-a-kind wine from the regions of Chinon and Bourgueil. Often slightly light in color, with moderate tannins, the wines have potent aromas of blackberry, plums, earth, and tobacco, plus a strong yet pleasing bell pepper note.

Wine and Grape Varieties Cheat Sheet

Many famous wines of the world do not mention grapes on the label because their region of origin is governed by wine laws that dictate exactly which grapes can be grown and used in wine. Think of this as a consumer protection initiative: every time you buy a bottle, you know exactly what you are getting—at least as far as grape variety is concerned. But although these laws may guarantee what goes into the bottle, quality definitely varies among producers (and from vintage to vintage!), so keep an eye out and do your research.

Here's a handy guide to the varieties of grape that correspond to well-known wine regions and styles.

REGION/STYLE	GRAPE
Beaujolais	gamay
Bordeaux	cabernet sauvignon, merlot, and cabernet franc
Burgundy	chardonnay for white wines, pinot noir for red wines
Chablis	chardonnay
Champagne	blend of chardonnay, pinot noir, and meunier
Châteauneuf-du-Pape	grenache-based blend
Chianti Classico	sangiovese
Pouilly-Fuissé	chardonnay
Pouilly-Fumé	sauvignon blanc
Rioja	tempranillo
Sancerre	sauvignon blanc
Vouvray	chenin blanc

Dry vs. Sweet Wines

During the fermentation stage of wine making, yeast converts grape sugars into alcohol (see page 32). How much sugar remains, if any, determines whether the wine is sweet, dry, or somewhere in between. The winemaker controls how much of the sugar the yeast eats by halting yeast action, either by chilling the wine, adding sulphur, fortifying the wine with grape spirit, or removing the yeast.

At one end of the spectrum are *dry wines*. These have little to no perceptible sugar or sweetness on the palate because the yeast ate it all during fermentation. Dry wines make up the majority of wines on the market. Examples include chardonnay and sauvignon blanc. When the yeast eats most of the sugar during fermentation but a bit remains, the result is an *off-dry wine*, which has some noticeable residual sugar. German kabinett riesling or demi-sec Vouvray from the Loire Valley of France are two examples of off-dry wines. *Sweet wine* is what it sounds like. The yeasts ate very little of the sugar during fermentation, leaving a wine that feels richer on the palate. Sauternes from Bordeaux, France, and any wines labeled as "late harvest" are sweet wines.

Besides halting yeast action as described above, winemakers have a few other ways to make wines sweet, both in the vineyard and in the winery.

- **Late harvesting:** Leaving the grapes on the vine longer than normal, into fall and sometimes even winter, can be a dangerous gamble with Mother Nature, animals, pests, and disease. But the longer ripening time allows grape sugar to continue to increase and water in the grapes to evaporate, dehydrating the berries almost until they are raisins and leaving them full of concentrated sugar, which will then create a sweeter wine.

- **Using mold:** Yep, mold! *Botrytis cinerea* is a fungus that attacks grapes and other plants in humid environments. When used intentionally and properly, it sucks out all the water in the grapes without rendering the fruit unusable, leaving behind honey-like sugar that is ideal for making dessert wines. Tokaji aszú from Hungary, Sauternes from the Bordeaux region of France, and Germany's trockenbeerenauslese are examples of dessert wine made with the help of botrytis.

- **Drying:** Similar to the late-harvesting method, grapes can be hung from the rafters in the winery until they shrivel into raisins. Vin santo from Italy is a prime example of wine made this way.

- **Freezing:** Ice wine is made using grapes that are left on the vine into the winter until they freeze. The water in the fruit freezes, leaving behind a thick, rich, syrupy sugar, which has accumulated after many extra months on the vine. The grapes are hand-harvested—in the middle of the night, in the middle of winter—and then pressed to separate the sugar from the icy water. Because true ice wine is so labor-intensive, it is very expensive, but well worth it! When you find a bottle of $15 ice wine, know that the grapes were probably put into a freezer and pressed rather than being frozen on the vine.

- **Fortifying:** Wine was once fortified, or strengthened with neutral grape alcohol (clear brandy), in order to preserve it during long ship voyages. Fortified wines continue to be produced to honor their deep-rooted tradition. When fortification occurs during fermentation, a high-octane spirit is added to grape juice, killing the yeasts and often producing a sweeter style of wine with greater alcohol content (in the 17 to 22 percent range). Port, sweet styles of madeira such as

Malmsey, and French Vins Doux Naturels such as Muscat de Beaumes de Venise or Banyuls are examples of wines fortified during fermentation. Alternatively, fortification may occur after the wine has fermented to dryness; this method is used for dry styles of sherry and madeira.

Don't be afraid of a little sugar. Sweet wines are some of the favorites among the pros because they are delicious and pair well with so many types of food (see page 106 for more), not just desserts.

Why You Should Love Wine Blends

Quite often I hear people insist "I don't like blends!" but any true wine snob knows not to fall into that trap. These days, blends are all the rage. Have you noticed in the wine shop how many wines have interesting, if not downright amusing, brand names with eye-catching labels that make no mention of a single grape variety? Nine out of ten times these are blends. In fact, many of the great wines of the world, such as those from Champagne, Bordeaux, the Rhône Valley, Rioja, and even many of the cult reds from California and Washington state modeled after the wines of Bordeaux, are traditionally made as blends. Here's what to know about these hybrid wines:

- Blends are a good bet. Two ideas are at work with blending, and they often go hand in hand: tradition, for one, and also the practicalities of grape growing. From a farming perspective, growing multiple varieties that flower and ripen at different times can protect against losing an entire crop when nature deals a heavy blow like early- or late-season frosts, ferocious winds, and intense rain. Diversifying provides a little insurance against all-out loss.

- **Blends can be constant companions.** Certain grape varieties love to be blended, like sauvignon blanc with sémillon, or grenache paired with Syrah. These BFF grapes help make each other better (or make up for what the other lacks) and generally yield a wine that's greater than the sum of its parts. Multiple grape varieties may be fermented together in the same vessel or, more commonly, fermented separately and then blended. Many wineries will grow dozens of plots of the same variety, ferment them separately, and then blend the best resulting wines.

- **Blends have rules.** In the United States, a wine must contain a minimum amount of the grape variety noted on the label—75 percent if the label mentions a state or county, like California or Sonoma Valley, 85 if it identifies an American Viticultural Area (AVA) such as Napa Valley AVA—meaning that 15 to 25 percent of the bottle is anyone's guess. (The exception is Oregon, where a minimum of 90 percent is required for pinot noir, pinot gris, riesling, chardonnay, and a few others. For grapes that are traditionally blended, such as cabernet sauvignon, merlot, and others, a minimum of 75 percent is required.)

How Wine Is Aged

In spite of the popular saying, not *all* wine gets better with age. Some, like most pinot grigio or riesling, are unaged and are bottled soon after fermentation in stainless-steel tanks that impart no flavor and preserve the grape variety's clean, fresh, youthful aromas and flavors. However, aging in oak barrels is a time-honored tradition that allows slow, gentle oxidation to occur as air enters the barrel, which rounds out and softens the texture. Oak aging also intensifies flavor because the wood allows some of the water in the wine to evaporate. But it's far from a mysterious process: here's everything you need to know.

- Old vs. new: Brand-new oak (or "first use") barrels impart a great deal of flavor and tannin to wine. As the barrels are used for successive vintages, their potency wanes, and by the fourth or fifth year the barrel is rendered neutral. It no longer imparts flavor but instead gives a more oxidative (i.e., nuttier and rounder) note and a textural change on the palate.

- Barrel size: In some wine regions, aging typically occurs in very large oak barrels called *foudres* that range in size from 1,500 liters to 10,000 (!) liters. These vessels impart only a very subtle flavor to the wine, because so little of the liquid comes in contact with the wood, and cause some oxidation, creating a rounder, smoother texture. The smaller barrel size most common for the wines of Bordeaux and many richly styled cabernet sauvignon and cabernet-based blends from California is called a *barrique*. Their relatively large surface-area-to-wine ratio imparts the most aroma and flavor. As a result, these barrels are very expensive, and many wineries use a high proportion of new barrels each year—which is just one of many reasons these wines might come with a high price tag.

- Wood types: Different types of oak impart different aromas and flavors. French oak, which costs about $850 per barrel or more, is more fine-grained and contributes subtler flavors of vanilla, toast, and spice. American oak, usually about $400 per barrel, is looser-grained and imparts more intense aromas and flavors of dill, coconut, and vanilla extract.

- **The oak chip shortcut.** If oak barrels are so expensive, how do cheap wines get such oaky flavors? Many wineries drop oak chips into wine as an inexpensive alternative to barrel aging. They give a similar flavor at a fraction of the cost.

Vintage 101

When you hear wine lovers raving about the 1982 Château Latour, they're talking about vintage. A wine's vintage simply refers to the year the grapes were harvested. And in wine making, as in life, some years are better than others. Even the most seasoned farmers must contend with frost, hail, strong winds, strong storms, flooding, or drought, which can cause growers to lose their entire crop. When a harvest takes a big hit, there are very few grapes to make wine, meaning production plummets—and, usually, the price will skyrocket. Especially in marginal growing areas, where ripening is more difficult, yearly weather has even greater potential to make or break the yield.

And it's not just the yield that's affected by the growing season. Just as the tomatoes in your garden don't taste exactly the same every year, the quality of grapes that make wine can vary widely depending on the conditions they're grown in. The grapes can get sun-burned in extreme heat, bloated and diluted by too much rain, shattered off the vine by hail, or killed in a frost.

Given these many variables that can make or break a given year's harvest, a perfect season is rare, especially in areas with significant weather fluctuations. Places like California are nice: they have pretty consistent weather, aside from the drought and forest fires. But northerly parts of Europe are much more temperamental, so each vintage is a unique reflection of how the winemakers fared with what nature gave them. If the grapes are sub-par because the weather is horrible, winemakers cannot make high-quality wine. They can do their best, of course, but the inherent quality will not be there. The characteristics of the wine change, the yields change based on what happened—and the prices change, too.

Yet, despite the significance of vintage, you won't always see a year on the label—some bottles, such as a blend of wines produced in two different years, don't have a vintage. Also keep in mind that two bottles of the same wine from the same vintage may take on very different qualities depending on how well they're stored and aged. Want to learn about the difference firsthand? Host a tasting (see page 114) and compare two vintages of a similar wine.

How Champagne (and Other Bubbly) Gets Its Sparkle

Perfect for celebrations (or just celebrating every day), sparkling wines can be sweet or dry, and red, white, or pink. Where the carbon dioxide gas created during fermentation of still wine is released into the atmosphere, in sparkling wine it is retained via one of the following methods, giving bubbly its characteristic fizz.

TRADITIONAL METHOD

The most famous and the highest-quality method for making sparkling wine was invented—and is championed—by the winemakers of Champagne, France (and until recently it was known as the *méthode champenoise*, or Champagne method). This method is used to make a variety of well-known sparkling wines, including cava, Crémant de Bourgogne, Crémant d'Alsace, Franciacorta, and sparkling wines from many excellent producers in California, Oregon, and Washington state.

1. Base wine/primary fermentation: To start the process, the base wine is fermented in the normal fashion (see page 32). In the Champagne region, three grape varieties are traditionally used: chardonnay, pinot noir, and meunier (which is tough to grow outside of this region, so it is rarely used in sparklers made elsewhere).

2. Secondary fermentation: The base wine is bottled with a mixture of additional sugar and yeast called *liqueur de tirage* and is closed with a crown cap (like the kind used on beer bottles). The bottles are rested on their sides for up to eight weeks as the yeast slowly converts the added sugar to alcohol and carbon dioxide.

3. Aging on the lees: This is where the magic happens. After the yeast has converted all of the sugar, the yeast cells break down and form sediment, or lees. The wine will be aged "on the lees" for a period that is often dictated by law in European countries (for example, Champagne requires a minimum of twelve months for non-vintage bottlings). Most producers far exceed the minimum, however, because it is during this process that the signature flavors of baked bread, brioche, and fresh dough are cre-

ated. More time on the lees also intensifies texture, creating finer bubbles.

4. **Riddling:** By this point, each bottle has a bunch of dead yeast cells floating around in it, which need to be removed so people don't have white gunk floating in their beautiful glass of expensive Champagne. The bottles are placed into racks pointed downward, so the sediment collects in the neck of the bottle. (The first such racks were invented by Madame Clicquot, for whom Veuve Clicquot Champagne is named.)

5. **Disgorgement:** With the bottle pointed straight down, the neck of the bottle is frozen in a solution. Then the bottle cap is flipped off, and the built-up pressure in the bottle ejects the frozen yeast.

6. **Dosage:** After the yeast is removed, another solution of wine and sugar is added to top off the bottle and adjust the flavor of the wine, either to soften the acidity or to achieve a desired sweetness. The dosage determines the final style of the wine. The word *brut* on the label indicates a dry style of Champagne, and *demi-sec* indicates a sweeter style.

CHARMAT METHOD

The traditional method of making sparkling wine takes many months or years and is quite labor-intensive and expensive because the bubbles are created in the individual bottle. The Charmat method takes much less time and is less costly. The process begins the same, with the creation of a base wine, but instead of undergoing secondary fermentation in individual bottles, the bubbles are created in pressurized tanks, which takes four to five days. The wine is filtered and then bottled under pressure. The bubbles created using this method are not so fine as those produced in the traditional method, but the cost and time savings (as little as ninety days from harvest to bottle) makes these wines an excellent value. It's used for fresher, fruiter styles of sparkling wine, like prosecco and even some Moscato d'Asti.

NOT ALL "CHAMPAGNE" IS CHAMPAGNE

All wine snobs know that Champagne comes only from the Champagne region of France. In the European Union, labeling laws are incredibly strict—plus, the *champenois* will send a cease-and-desist letter to anyone who dares to call their sparkling wine Champagne. By EU law, all other sparkling wines—even those made using the same process—must use a different name, such as Crémant (the term for other French sparklers). Not only that, sparkling-wine producers cannot even use the words "Champagne method" on a label; instead, they must say "traditional" or "classic" method.

So why do you see new world wines using the term Champagne? Outside the EU, such standards don't exist. The current rule in the United States allows existing "Champagne" producers to continue labeling their wines as they always have, but prevents *new* producers from using EU-protected place names (including Champagne, but also Chablis, Burgundy, Port, and others).

Why Does Wine Get So Expensive?

Even for the seasoned wine snob, the price tag on some bottles can be eye-popping. Wine producers have specific intentions for the kind of wine they want to produce, all of which can affect price: Is the focus on quality or quantity? Is the wine destined to be sold in a gallon jug for under ten bucks, a large-scale brand by a rockstar winemaker, or a selection of only a few hundred cases from one of the best small vineyards? Then there's the simple economics of production: the cost of grapes, tanks and barrels for aging, corks, labels, and bottles, plus labor costs. (And here you may have thought wine making was super romantic, right?) Here is a little insight into the financial perspective of wine making.

- Location of vineyards: In order to grow grapes, you need quality real estate. A vineyard owner buying land in the Napa Valley may spend nearly half a million dollars an acre; in the very top vineyards of Burgundy, France, plots of land are valued in the millions of euros. With vineyard and land prices in these stratospheres, you probably won't stay in business very long selling your wine for $10 a bottle! So-called value wines come from peripheral vineyards and/or up-and-coming areas. Many large-production wineries, those making millions of cases per year, keep costs down by sourcing fruit from vast tracts of land in less desirable areas.

- Yields: Grape growers can choose how much a vine produces, letting it grow freely (which results in more bunches with less concentrated flavor) or limiting the number of bunches by cutting them off the vine and dropping them to the ground (aka "green harvesting"), which yields fewer grapes with a higher intensity of flavor in the fruit and the resulting wine. The fewer grapes grown, the more expensive they'll be.

- Barrels: Aging in new oak is costly. A single barrel from a top French producer can cost $1,500 to $2,000 or more. Depending on production volume and how many new barrels are purchased per year (since the barrels lose their potency with time; see page 57), this is a significant expense for the winery that will trickle down to the price of the bottle.

- Supply, demand, and branding: Some "cult" wines (especially from California) cost exorbitant amounts of money simply because people will pay it. If a respected wine reviewer gives a wine a great score, the demand for it will skyrocket—along with the price. Some wines, namely from a few well-known areas in France, are expensive because they always have been expensive: no matter the quality of the vintage, the price will still be high. (Don't get me wrong—great care goes into making these wines, but supply is adequate, and these prices have as much to do with maintaining a brand image as with quality.) Finally, scarcity can be powerful. Some of the most expensive wines on earth cost a lot because just a few bottles are produced.

SO IS EXPENSIVE
WINE BETTER?

I am often asked what the difference is between a $100 bottle and a $10 bottle, but in the end it's truly subjective—not just in terms of taste or quality, but also in terms of the value of the experience or, perhaps, the emotional significance of a particular wine to a person. I'm not one to spend $500 on a pair of shoes, but many of my friends do and that's fine by me. When it comes to wine, spend as much as you want, and try not to judge others.

Special Labels: Kosher, Organic, and Biodynamic Wine

As with many things in the world of wine, the words on the label matter. Wines labeled as kosher, organic, or biodynamic all must be made with specific steps, restrictions, or specifications to make them meet the standards of their designation. Here's what makes each of them unique.

KOSHER WINE

Wine is very important in the Jewish faith and tradition and, like food, it is governed by strict dietary laws. For a wine to be considered kosher, religious or Sabbath-observant Jews supervise and sometimes handle the entire wine-making process, from the crushing of the grapes and fermentation to bottling and even serving. Only kosher ingredients can be used throughout the process, including finings, which are additives that clarify wine.

In the shop, kosher wines bear a seal of approval on the bottle with the Ⓚ or Ⓤ symbol administered by an approved kosher certification organization. Kosher wine is also flash-pasteurized so it may be deemed *mevushal*, or suitable to be handled and poured by any nonreligious person. In this process, the wine is heated to 160°F for 30 seconds and then immediately chilled back to room temperature, a process that's said to have a minimal effect on flavor.

In the United States, the most notable brands are Manischewitz and Mogen David, both made from Concord grapes, members of the species *Vitis labrusca*. You may recognize the distinctively sweet and musky flavor of this native northeastern American grape variety from grape jelly (or grape-flavored Bubblicious!).

Many wine-producing countries including Israel, France, Germany, Italy, and Australia make delicious, high-quality kosher *Vitis vinifera* wines. In addition, quite a few famous Champagne houses and Bordeaux châteaus produce separate kosher bottlings of popular styles from dedicated winemakers.

ORGANIC WINE

Sustainability has become increasingly relevant in wine culture conversations as wineries seek to promote the long-term health of the soil and improve the relationship of the vineyard and winery to its environment. Organic winemaking is just one facet of the complex issue of sustainability, which can also incorporate planting decisions, water usage, waste management, energy efficiency, recycling, carbon footprint, pest control, and even labor practices.

In the United States, a wine that is labeled as organic has been produced from organically grown grapes (i.e., grapes grown without pesticides) and contains no added sulfites. (In Europe and Canada, organic wines may contain sulfites.) The latter specification precludes many quality wines from this classification because so many rely on sulfites as a preservative and to prevent oxidation and a host of microbial problems (see page 75). Instead, many U.S. wines are labeled with the phrase "made from organically grown grapes," which permits the addition of sulfites up to 100 parts per million (about half the amount in a typical serving of dried apricots). Additionally, *organic* refers only to how the grapes are grown, not the rest of the winemaking process. And with the exception of sulfites, the wine may contain other additives.

BIODYNAMIC WINE

Introduced by the Austrian philosopher Rudolf Steiner in 1924 and championed today by winemaker Nicolas Joly of the Loire Valley in France, biodynamic viticulture is a belief system that takes the concepts of organic and sustainable farming a step further into the seemingly mystical realms of the rhythms and forces of the Earth. Farming—in this case, grape growing—is tied not only to the success of the ecosystem as a whole but also to the cosmos, all of which unite to become one organism that generates its own fertility by the cycle of seasons and the moon. Biodynamic vineyard workers time their tasks according to the movement of celestial bodies, particularly the moon. Homeopathic mixtures produced from animal and mineral substances like dandelion flowers, stinging nettles, and "horn manure" (a manure-stuffed cow's horn that is buried in the vineyard) are used to treat and heal the soil. Biodynamic viticulture can be a controversial topic, particularly in more traditional circles.

The Truth about Sulfites

How many times have you heard someone say, "I can't drink red wine because I'm allergic to sulfites"? These chemical compounds tend to get a bad rap for causing negative reactions in wine drinkers. Let's separate fact from fiction and find out what really is causing those headaches.

Sulfites are used in wine making to keep harmful bacterial or fungal organisms from growing and spoiling the wine. (These substances' preservative qualities are also used to keep dried fruits pristine—compare brown unsulfured apricots to the bright, plump pink-orange ones, which have been sulfured.) They also have an antioxidant effect and prevent wine from turning brown (yuck). Sweeter wines often contain more sulfites than drier wines to prevent spoilage or refermentation (when microscopic yeast cells hanging around on the bottle or cork or in the wine begin a new fermentation—not good!). And although red wine usually gets the blame, often white wines contain higher levels of sulfites than reds.

Sulfite intolerance reportedly affects less than 1 percent of the population and usually manifests like a standard allergic reaction, with symptoms such as hives, runny nose, sneezing, and asthma. A mild headache—or hangover—does not necessarily indicate sulfite intolerance.

The sulfite stigma likely stems from the legal requirement that all wines containing sulfites prominently display that fact on every bottle. However, many foods and drugs on the market have much higher levels of sulfites—but they are not required to say so prominently on the label. (It will, however, be listed among the ingredients.) Other foods that contain sulfites include bottled (not frozen) lemon or lime juice, molasses, sauerkraut and its juice, grape juices (white, white sparkling, pink sparkling, red sparkling), and pickled cocktail onions. If you are not allergic to any of these high-sulfite foods, you are probably not allergic to sulfites in wine!

In addition to requiring that the presence of sulfites be indicated on the label, the USDA limits the sulfite content of specific wine categories, as shown in the chart opposite.

TYPE OF WINE	SULFITES (parts per million)
Organic wine*	10 ppm naturally occurring sulfite (yes, organic wines contain sulfites!)
Biodynamic wine	100 ppm added sulfite
Wine "made with organic grapes"	150 ppm added sulfite
All wine	350 ppm added sulfite

*Note that the EU allows wines labeled organic to contain 100 to 150 parts per million of sulfites, depending on the variety.

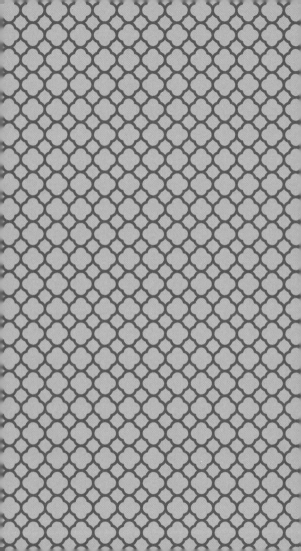

DRINK
UP

How to Read a Wine Label

You can't judge a book by its cover, but can you tell what a wine tastes like by reading the label? Yes, most of the time. However, being able to do so with ease takes a good amount of experience and knowledge of wine regions, the grape varieties grown in particular places, and the styles of wines made from those grapes. (In other words, you just gotta taste more wine!) To get you started, here's a rundown of what you can—and cannot—learn from reading a wine label.

- Specific, protected styles. All those strict laws in European wine regions protect a place and style of wine. With a little knowledge of protected styles (see page 66) you can get a sense of the wine before popping the cork. So when you see a bottle of white Sancerre, you know generally what kind of wine you're getting: the wine was made from sauvignon blanc grapes; it is crisp, dry, tart, and citrusy; it may have a bit of grassy or green-pepper flavor that is typical of that grape variety; and it has no impression of oak.

(Of course, despite the legal definitions of wine styles, every vintage year is different, and there is variance in quality among producers.)

- Alcohol content. The alcohol level will tell you how potent the wine is, of course, but will also give an indication of the body and potential sweetness. Wines that are greater than 14 percent alcohol by volume (ABV) are considered full-bodied and can be quite rich and intense. Wines with less than 12 percent ABV are lighter in body. If the ABV is below 10 or 11 percent, there is a good chance the wine may have residual sugar.

- Climate and terroir. If you can imagine the region's geographic location and determine if the climate is generally cool, warm, or hot, you may be able to get a sense of the style of the wine. Remember, climate determines ripeness of the fruit—the more sugar ripeness in the fruit, the more potential richness in flavor and more potential alcohol. Wines from cool climates generally will have tarter and leaner characteristics and lower alcohol, whereas wines from warm to hot wine regions will have riper fruit flavors, elevated alcohol, and usually less tartness (depending on the grape variety). Of course there are many exceptions and anomalies, but this is a good rule of thumb to start with.

- **Target audience.** A label with cartoons, a goofy name, or a zany font indicates that the wine-maker is probably trying to reach a newer or less experienced clientele—not that there's anything wrong with that!—so the wine may be more fruity and sweet. An artsy, but still modern, label is likely aiming up the ladder in terms of wine snobbery. Classic château labels typically are geared toward seasoned drinkers, but since the look has become shorthand for "prestige," you may see them on bargain-priced wines, too.

One thing you cannot tell from a label: personal preference. If the producer is unfamiliar to you, nothing printed on the front of the bottle will indicate if you are going to like the wine it contains. In that case, there's only one way to find out . . .

How to Open a Wine Bottle

Getting handy with a corkscrew (or comfortable popping the bubbly!) is a wine snob rite of passage. Here's how to crack open the good stuff without putting an eye out. (Not sure which kind of corkscrew you have? Check page 121.)

OPENING WITH A WINGED CORKSCREW

1. Remove foil from the bottle and lower the two arms (aka "wings") of the corkscrew.

2. Place the ring over the cork.

3. Turn the top tab of the corkscrew so that the screw (or "worm") digs in to the cork. Keep turning until the wings are all the way up.

4. Push down the wings. The cork should lift out of the bottle as the worm rises.

OPENING WITH A WAITER'S FRIEND CORKSCREW

1. Cut the foil off the bottle at the second lip (i.e., the bottom of the wider part near the spout) using the small knife attachment.

2. Unfold the corkscrew and twist the worm down into the center of the cork until just one ring of the worm is still showing.

3. Rest the first level of the lever (the one nearest the hinge) on the neck of the bottle at the top lip. Gently pull up once.

4. Use the next notch of the lever to gently pull the cork out of the bottle, taking care to keep the hinge in alignment to avoid bending or breaking the cork.

OPENING SPARKLING WINE

1. Loosen the metal cage around the cork by twisting it a few times. It should be loose enough to pass over the bottle's lip, but don't remove it just yet!

2. Place a dishtowel over the bottle's neck, in case of spills or accidental premature cork popping.

3. Angle the bottle about 45 degrees. Hold the cork and cage in place with one hand while rotating the bottom of the bottle with the other. (Don't rotate the cork!)

4. Continue turning the bottle and letting the cork out a little at a time until you hear the tell-tale pop and fizz.

Glassware 101

There are types of glassware on the market for every single style of wine (not to mention beers and spirits). Each piece is designed to enhance specific aromas and flavors in wine, and having nice glasses for enjoying nice bottles of wine is a treat. However, one or two styles really can cover all occasions, and you don't need to spend a fortune (though you certainly can!). Don't spend so much that you want to cry when one eventually breaks. Knowing the different styles will help you pick the best wineglasses for you.

CARE AND CLEANING OF GLASSWARE

Wash glasses by hand with mild soap and buff dry with a clean, lint-free cloth. You can wash glasses in the dishwasher, but use caution—avoid harsh cleaners and don't overload the machine with glasses or other heavy items, which may cause breakage. Before every use, polish your glasses one last time with hot water or steam to get rid of any water stains or odors from the cabinet they were stored in.

ALL-PURPOSE

All-purpose glass: This is the glass I use most often, for everyday drinking and for wine evaluation. This glass is perfect for light- to medium-bodied white wines like sauvignon blanc, riesling, and pinot grigio. (I even use them for beer and Champagne!) If you entertain at home, I recommend having a dozen or two of these on hand for parties.

CHAMPAGNE FLUTE

Champagne flute: This tall, slim glass provides a festive and enjoyable view of sparkling wines' *perlage*, or bubbles, as they rise. The slim glass also concentrates the aromas to the forefront and retains the bubbles longer than a wider, more spacious glass.

BURGUNDY

Burgundy glass: Also known as a bowl glass, this is most often used for fuller-bodied whites and lighter reds. It is meant for the Burgundy grape varieties of chardonnay and pinot noir, but it also works beautifully for some northern Italian red wines like Barolo or Barbaresco and Barbera.

BORDEAUX

Bordeaux glass: As the name implies, this glass is ideal for full-bodied reds, such as cabernet sauvignon and merlot. However, any wine that is big and brawny will do well in this glass; I enjoy it for rioja, malbec, and Shiraz.

STEMLESS

Mason jars, stemless glasses, and tumblers: The wide base of these glasses enhances aromas and flavors. Stemless glasses work for any occasion, but the plastic ones are great for big parties (read: no broken glass). The only downside is fingerprints on the glass, but if you hate finicky cleanup, it's a good tradeoff!

How to Pour a Proper Glass of Wine

There's more to consider when filling your glass than how much you want to drink and how few trips you want to make back to the serving area. First, set your glass on a table—wine bottles can be difficult to balance with one hand. A true wine snob knows not to pour wine by grabbing the neck of the bottle. Pouring with a thumb in the punt (the indentation at the bottom of the bottle) isn't so great, either, because it affords you little control of the bottle, increasing the likelihood of dropping it or spilling the wine (nooo!). For the best grip, grasp the bottle in the middle, near the label.

A proper pour is about two-thirds or less of the glass. This helps keep the unpoured wine at the right temperature in the bottle and also leaves room in the glass for you to swirl the wine and enjoy the aromas.

For sparkling wines, hold the glass in one hand and the bottle in the other, again grasping in the middle. Tilt the glass and pour wine along the side, not directly to the bottom, to slow the rate at which the wine flows out (thereby preserving the bubbles).

The Perfect Serving Temperature for Any Style

TYPE OF WINE	TEMPERATURE
Sweet white	42°F–50°F
Champagne and sparkling	42°F–50°F
Light- and medium-bodied white (riesling, sauvignon blanc)	42°F–50°F
Dry rosé	45°F–55°F
Full-bodied white (viognier, chardonnay)	50°F–59°F
Light-bodied red wine (gamay)	50°F–59°F
Medium-bodied red (pinot noir, cabernet franc)	55°F–62°F
Full-bodied red (cabernet sauvignon, zinfandel, Syrah)	58°F–65°F

HOW TO MEASURE TEMPERATURE

Use an infrared thermometer that measures liquid temperatures (fancy!) or estimate relative to room and fridge temperature.

68°F	Room temperature
59°F–65°F	Slightly below room temperature
55°F–62°F	Slightly chilled
50°F–59°F	Chilled
45°F–55°F	Cold, somewhat above refrigerator temperature
42°F–50°F	Cold, slightly above refrigerator temperature
35°F–45°F	Refrigerator temperature
32°F	Freezing

To get your wine at the right temperature, place the bottle in the fridge or freezer (don't forget about it!) to chill and then return it to room temperature so that it warms up just enough, in either the glass or the bottle. But be careful with full-bodied reds: serving them too cold brings out their tannins.

How to Taste Wine Like a Pro

Point of order: There is no *wrong* way to taste wine. If you drink it and enjoy it, you're doing it right. Still, the true wine snob wants to savor the experience for maximum enjoyment. Here are the steps to get the most out of every glass.

1. **Hold the glass.** Ever see a movie or TV show in which the "wine expert" character holds the wineglass by the bowl? No good! For one thing, you can easily break the glass in your grip, especially if it's delicate. Also, wouldn't you rather see the pretty wine than the greasy fingerprints you left on the glass after eating that canapé? Instead, use your thumb and first two fingers to hold the glass near the base of the stem.

2. **Consider the color.** First, tilt the glass away from you (pros do it against a white background) to take in all of the colors in the wine. (Raising the glass can be effective as well, but don't spill it!) Look at the concentration of the color, which can be a clue to how the wine was made—for

example, a white wine that is older or has been aged in oak takes on a deeper golden hue. Color can also indicate the grape variety used. Pinot noir and nebbiolo, for example, have very little pigmentation in their skins and therefore generally produce light-colored wines. Cabernet sauvignon and Syrah (Shiraz), by contrast, have a boatload of pigmentation and generally produce darker-colored wines.

3. **Eye the tears.** Some wine snobs extol the virtues of a wine's "tears" or "legs"—the streaks that slide down the sides of the glass after swirling. But legs don't indicate quality so much as the amount of alcohol, sugar, or dry extract in the wine reacting to both the oxygen in the air and the surface of the glass, thereby creating surface tension. The science is a little complicated, but in the end, the legs can be a useful visual tool to gauge alcohol content: wines that are higher in alcohol form more legs that are slow-moving, and those lower in alcohol have legs that are less distinct and dissipate more quickly.

4. **Smell.** Describing a wine's "nose" is essentially a two-step process:

- Swirl: With your fingers at the base of the glass, move the glass in a controlled circle (don't worry—the wine doesn't care which direction you choose). This may seem like a fancy-schmancy wine snob thing to do, but it serves a purpose: swirling helps volatilize the aromatic compounds (geek speak for bringing aromas to the surface so they're more easily smelled). Until you get the hang of it, practice with white wine or water—not red wine!—for easier cleanup in case of a spill.

- Sniff: This isn't a delicate "wave the glass in front of your nose" situation: stick your nose way in and deeply inhale with your mouth slightly open. It's okay if at first you don't smell anything but plain old wine! With practice you'll be able to translate the physiological sensation into words. (Wine pros spend time in the produce and bulk-spice aisles of grocery stores to practice smelling and verbalizing what they detect.) If you're new to discerning the aromas in wine, try thinking in broad categories to start (like earthy or fruity) and get more specific with time. The questions on the next page may help.

AROMA EVALUATION:
ASPECTS TO CONSIDER

Is the aroma subtle or intense?

Do you detect a scent of leather or dried and stewed fruit? These aromas strengthen with time and indicate age.

What fruit can you smell?

- In white wines: citrus, apple and pear, tropical fruits, or melon
- In red wines: cherries, raspberries, blackberries, plums, or blueberries

What non-fruit aromas do you notice?

- Earthy aromas: mushroom, forest floor, wet rocks
- Wood or oak barrel aromas: vanilla, toast, baking spices, dill, coconut
- Other aromas: flowers, cedar, tobacco

5. **Taste.** Finally! Take a small sip and swish the wine over all the surfaces of your mouth, including your gums and teeth. Then spit or swallow the wine and pause to consider. Your sense of taste combined with the aroma gives you the full experience of the wine's flavor. (Think of how nothing tastes right when you have a cold.) Consider the following key flavor components:

+ **Sweetness:** Remember how, back in the winery, the winemaker determined if the wine would be sweet or dry (see page 50)? Now you can taste the effects of that decision. Don't confuse sweet wine with wines that smell or taste fruity—here we're talking about the presence of real sugar.

+ **Acidity:** Acidity in wine is perceived as a sour or tart sensation that makes your mouth water—which is a good thing! Natural acidity in wine makes your mouth click with excitement: just think of how your mouth reacts when you eat a fresh orange or tangerine. The more your mouth waters, the better that wine will go with food. I bet your mouth is watering just thinking about it! A wine with low acidity feels dull and flabby on the palate, with no liveliness. It will sit on your palate almost like flat soda. A wine in balance with acidity will keep you wanting to drink more and keep your palate refreshed.

- **Tannins:** The amount of tannin depends on the genetics of the grape variety. Tannin presents itself in wine as a drying-out sensation on the palate, which is associated with bitterness. (Where tartness makes your mouth water, bitterness makes your mouth dry.) Imagine drinking over-steeped black tea and the sensation of dryness that would create in your mouth.

- **Body:** Body is a perception of how heavily the wine weighs on your palate. The higher the alcohol content of a wine, the fuller the body (and, conversely, the lower the alcohol, the lighter the body). Sugar in wine also gives roundness and the perception of body even when the alcohol level is low.

- **Textures:** This refers to how the wine physically feels on your palate: round, lean, oily, creamy, rough, and so on. These sensations may result from the grape variety or how the wine was made.

- Flavors: Review the aromas you smelled in step 4. Can you detect similar flavors when you taste it? What about anything new and different? Is the wine fruitier or tarter than expected?

6. **Evaluate and record.** Once you've had a thorough taste, it's time to decide how you feel about this wine. What do you like or dislike? Use as many of the terms above as you can—practicing how to describe what you like (or don't like!) will help you find the wine that best suits your tastes when in restaurants and wine shops. And whether you take a picture with your phone or keep a label scrapbook, record what you've tasted for reference in future tasting endeavors.

How to Age and Cellar Wine

To drink now or to cellar? Ninety-nine percent of the wine on the market is meant to be drunk now, not cellared and aged. That said, some wines fit the old adage and indeed improve with age. These usually have one or more of the following attributes (which act as natural preservatives) that lead to graceful aging.

- High natural acidity: Think Champagne or German riesling from top vintages, or the great red and white wines of Burgundy, France.

- High sugar content: These include the top dessert wines of the world, including Tokaji from Hungary and Sauternes from the Bordeaux region of France.

- Elevated tannin levels: Examples include Barolo and Barbaresco from northeastern Italy and red Bordeaux from the Médoc's top producers, like the great châteaux Lafite, Latour, and Haut-Brion.

- **High alcohol:** Top examples of fortified wines, like vintage port, are able to age for decades.

- **Already aged or oxidized:** Some wines are aged at the winery before release and can stand the test of time, such as Madeira or Rioja from top producers.

Once you've selected wines for aging, it's time to think about the space where you'll store them. Do you have room in your home or a storage facility to put the wine? Will you be buying more than you can possibly drink? If you're loading up on pricey bottles, having proper storage for your investment is a must to keep the wine in good condition for maximum enjoyment.

CELLARING DON'TS

Never store wine . . .

- Near a direct source of light that can cause UV damage to the wine

- In excessive heat or an area of extreme temperature fluctuation

- Near a source of vibration (like a big stereo speaker or a rattling pipe)

- In damp conditions, like a basement—you want humidity (see below), but not mold and mildew

- Near any source of unpleasant odors

CELLARING DOS

Always store wine . . .

- At a constant temperature of about 50°F–60°F

- According to an organized and an easy-to-access method

- With the bottles on their side to avoid corking (however, fortified wines should be stored standing up)

- In a location with around 70 percent humidity to keep corks from cracking (invest in a dehumidifier if your storage location is too damp)

Bottles can be arranged according to your preference, as long as you can find what you want when you need it. Most collectors arrange their wines by color and region to start, with further subdivisions by regions and producers. How much space you need depends on your aspirations as a collector. I have a collector friend who has a whole separate *house*, but you don't need to go that far. My first "cellar" consisted of bottles lying on a blanket in the bottom of my clothes closet. Invest in racks if you'd like—most are an internet search or shopping trip away.

Additionally, there are many websites and apps that allow you to keep track of bottles in your collection and remind you when to drink them.

How to Navigate a Restaurant Wine List

Ordering wine in front of colleagues, family, or a date can be stressful. Here's what to do.

1. LOOK AT THE LIST.

Quickly skim the list to see if it has a definable theme, such as wines organized by region, grape variety, and/or style. The list should include much of the same information as the label (see page 80), and some lists also mention tasting notes or food pairings. Don't get bogged down in flowery language (what's a "daring" wine?): good wine lists make it easy for you to find something you like.

2. TAKE ADVANTAGE OF THE EXPERT.

No one knows the wine list better than the buyer or sommelier. Give 'em a chance! Their job is to elevate your dining experience, and the best ones listen to your tastes and budget when making a recommendation. You can take or leave the advice, but the sommelier may just steer you to your next favorite wine! And if there's a problem with the wine you order, it's totally okay to let the sommelier know.

3. CONSIDER ORDERING BY THE GLASS.

Wine-savvy restaurants create their selection of wines by the glass with a sense of pride—it's a reflection of the restaurant concept, maybe a little of their personal style, and a designated companion to the cuisine. At any restaurant I have ever worked in, my wine-by-the-glass program was a mini version of the wine list and a chance for my chef and me to figure out creative pairings to enhance the diners' experience.

4. KNOW THE SERVING SIZE.

Most restaurants serve 5- to 6-ounce pours. In a wine-savvy restaurant, it will be served in nice, oversized stemware, which might make it *look* like a smaller pour. But in reality, this enables the wine snob to swirl and sniff and enjoy to their heart's content.

5. WHAT IF YOU HATE IT?

Whether the wine objectively has gone bad or you subjectively are not enjoying it, alert the sommelier or waiter immediately. Most wine-savvy restaurants, or any restaurant interested in hospitality, will help you make a new selection and replace the bottle immediately (especially if they recommended it or the bottle is faulty). Don't feel bad—true pros will understand that it's no fun to force yourself through a bottle.

How to Pair Wine with Food

On the subject of food pairing, one of my fellow master sommeliers, Andrea Robinson, always says: "Give them the tools, not rules!" Sure, some pairings work better than others, but we all have personal preferences that shape how we feel about certain food and wine interactions. Pairings can expose you to foods you never used to care for or, conversely, help you appreciate a wine you never in a million years would have thought you'd like.

That said, I have one important rule: always eat and drink what you like, no matter what anyone else says! If it is good to you, that's all that matters. To take your pairings to the next level, here are some strategies.

COMPLEMENT

Take an element in the wine and match a similar element in the food (or vice versa). For example, serve a buttery and creamy chardonnay with a buttery and creamy dish like pasta alfredo or asparagus with hollandaise.

CONTRAST

Contrast or counterbalance an element in the food with an element in the wine (or vice versa), such as a creamy, rich dish with a tangy and tart wine.

BE SWITZERLAND

Go neutral and pick a wine and a dish that both have middle-of-the-road flavors and profiles (as opposed to something pungent, spicy, or unusual).

GO BY COLORS

Match the color of your food to the color of your wine! For example: green foods like spring vegetables with green wines that are light in color and youthful and have a vegetal, herbal, and green citrus character (like sauvignon blanc, Grüner Veltliner, or vinho verde from Portugal). Or try pink—I love the combination of salmon, beet salad, and rosé.

USE YOUR GEOGRAPHY

A good rule of thumb: what grows together goes together. Think about the origins of a dish and go for a wine from the same or a nearby region. Everyone knows the Europeans have got it going on with food and wine, and traditionally they grow or prepare food to pair with the wine of their region.

TRY A FOOLPROOF PAIR

Here are nine food and wine pairings every wine snob should try before they die.

French fries	+	Champagne
Foie gras	+	Sauternes
Sardines	+	fino sherry
Sushi	+	German riesling
Alba white truffle and egg pasta	+	Barolo or Barbaresco
Stinky cheeses	+	Alsatian gewürztraminer
Salmon	+	pinot noir
Croque monsieur	+	French rosé
Roasted lamb	+	Bordeaux

REMEMBER THE SECRET THIRD ELEMENT

Ever find yourself enjoying a food and wine pairing without being able to explain the exact reason why? Often, a dining experience has more to do with the people you're with and the experience as a whole. Not to be all "the secret ingredient is love!" but truly, such experiences will resonate more strongly than pairings memorized from a book.

6 Classic Wine Cocktails

Of course, nothing beats an unadulterated glass of your favorite wine, but every wine snob should know at least a few classic combinations for when the occasion strikes.

KIR

This aperitif takes its name from Félix Kir, former mayor of Dijon, Burgundy, who used to serve it to guests.

To make: In a white-wine glass, combine $^1/_3$ ounce of crème de cassis with 3 ounces of white wine (such as Bourgogne Aligoté or Chablis). For a kir royale, use a champagne flute and substitute Champagne for white wine.

FRENCH 75

Invented circa World War I, this lemony gin-and-Champagne combination is named for the French 75-millimeter field gun because its alcoholic punch is just *that* strong.

To make: In a champagne flute, combine 1 ounce of gin, 2 dashes of simple syrup, $^1/_2$ ounce of lemon juice, and 2 ounces of Champagne.

MIMOSA

The brunch cocktail par excellence, this juice-and-Champagne combo is a beloved companion to everything from waffles to eggs Benedict.

To make: In a champagne flute, combine $2^1/_2$ ounces of Champagne and $2^1/_2$ ounces of orange juice.

BELLINI

The mimosa's peachy cousin, this cocktail hails from Venice, Italy, and is another morning favorite to accompany a late breakfast.

To make: In a champagne flute, combine $3^1/_2$ ounces of prosecco with $1^1/_2$ ounces of peach purée.

SANGRIA

The classic Spanish fruit-and-wine drink is easy to spin any way you'd like and perfect for pitchers to serve a crowd. Red wine or white, fruit as desired, optional brandy—there are no hard and fast rules.

To make: For traditional sangria, combine a 750-milliliter bottle of Spanish Rioja with 1 cup of orange juice, $1/4$ cup of sugar, and a few handfuls of chopped seasonal fruits (such as peaches, berries, apples, pears, and/or pineapple). For *sangria blanca*, substitute a bottle of dry Spanish white wine such as Rueda; if desired, add about $1/2$ cup of brandy, 2 cups of sparkling water, or both.

MULLED WINE

On cooler days, nothing beats a mug of warm and spicy mulled wine. Many European countries traditionally drink this beverage on Christmas.

To make: As with sangria, there's no master recipe, just a basic technique. To start, in a large pot combine a 750-milliliter bottle of red wine, 2 cups of port, 1 cup of apple cider, 1 whole cinnamon stick, and about 10 whole cloves. Add any other ingredients (such as chopped apples, sliced oranges, or additional spices like cardamom pods) to taste. Simmer over medium-low heat until warm, about 20 minutes.

LIVING
YOUR
WINE
SNOB
LIFE

How to Host a Wine Tasting Party

The best way to convert your friends into wine lovers is to have them taste a whole bunch of styles and see what the hype is all about. To make it a special occasion (and get the most out of your wine), don't invite everyone over for just a glass—host a bona fide tasting! Here's how to do it.

1. **Choose a format.** Do you want a guided, sit-down tasting or a walk-around event? Each one has its benefits—a guided tasting lets you share your expertise directly with guests while they taste, but the looser walk-around format allows people to sample at their own pace.

2. **Pick a theme.** Get creative with a theme that fits your style, budget, and occasion. The following are a few fun ways to explore new wines.

   • **By region:** Feature several wines from a single country or region. Examples: Italy (Wines of Tuscany), France (The Diversity of the Loire Valley), Greece (It's All Greek to Me!) or Down Under (New Zealand and Australia).

- **Wine and cheese:** Pair wines and cheeses from the same country (see "How to Pair Wine with Food" on page 106 for ideas).

- **By grape:** Explore the differences of wines made from the same grape grown in different regions—like chardonnay, sauvignon blanc, pinot noir, or riesling.

- **Old world vs. new world:** Similar to the previous theme, pick a few grape varieties to try in sets: French sauvignon blanc versus New Zealand sauvignon blanc, California chardonnay versus French chardonnay, Oregon pinot noir versus red Burgundy, Napa Cabernet versus Bordeaux, or sparkling wines from around the world.

- **Blind tasting competition:** Ask each guest to bring a bottle under a certain price point (say $15 or $20—nothing crazy). Wrap each bottle in foil or paper, and then number each one. Guests rate and pick their favorite wine of the group, and the winner has bragging rights until the next party.

- **Pairings 101:** Discover how basic elements in food interact with the flavors of wine. Put out small cups of sugar, salt, hot pepper sauce, butter, and smoky cheese or nuts, and encourage guests to compare each food to each wine. Pick a wide variety of wine styles to show how each food element pairs with them.

- Aroma exploration: Learning to identify aromas in wine is always daunting. To help guests with this task, set out the fruits, vegetables, and spices that certain wines are known to smell and taste like, alongside samples of the wine. For instance, if you're tasting a New Zealand sauvignon blanc, provide slices of grapefruit, lime, and jalapeño pepper for your guests to sniff and compare.

- Hire a sommelier! Having an expert on hand to help with all the details is an excellent way to take the pressure off the host. The sommelier can teach you blind tasting, walk you through a region, or suggest food and wine pairings.

3. Get your glassware. How much you need depends on the format of your tasting: about 2 glasses per person for a walk-around, or 1 glass per person per featured wine if you're sitting down and demonstrating one at a time. Many caterers rent nice wineglasses for just this kind

of occasion, or you can opt for plastic glassware and avoid the eventual broken-glass scenario. Note that quality glasses are not cheap or dishwasher safe, so hand-wash them after each use.

4. **Stock up on supplies.** Ice is a necessity, especially in summer months, to keep both white *and* red wines cool. Get a receptacle that can serve as a dump bucket. It doesn't have to be fancy; in the pro-wine world, we usually use a plastic bucket or even small ice tins. This will help guests feel free to try many wines without having to commit to full pours and drink more alcohol than they'd like—plus it's standard operating procedure at any professional wine tasting. Also have lots of water and food: bread, crackers, and cheese for during the tasting and heavier fare for after, to keep guests' tummies padded and balance the wine being tasted. Finally, wine charms (trinkets that distinguish your glass from someone else's) may seem cheesy, but they'll cut down on abandoned glasses and wasted wine. If you're going for a walk-around format, stock up on notecards or paper to display information about the grapes, wines, styles, vineyards, regions, etc.

5. **Buy enough wine.** Budget about 1 bottle per person, plus a little extra—so if you're inviting eight people, nine bottles will be about right. You may end up with leftover wine, but that's better than the alternative of running out of booze, especially if one of the bottles is off or bad.

6. **Pour and taste!** Serve small pours to start: it cuts down on waste, and guests can always have more if they want it. If your guests are new to tasting, you could demonstrate the proper technique described on page 93.

How to Bring the Perfect Wine for Any Occasion

Even for the seasoned snob, bringing wine to an event can be daunting, especially if the recipient is a fellow wine lover. What could they possibly want that they don't already have? Don't worry—you have plenty of options and do *not* have to blow your budget.

- **Know your audience.** If you know that your host likes a particular style or grape variety, ask a trusted expert at your local wine store for a recommendation in your price range. Remember: good wine doesn't have to be expensive. Half the fun of trying new wines is finding great value that exceeds your expectations. Besides, the person you're giving the bottle to doesn't need wine just to sit in their collection for months or years on end—they need wine for tonight, too! Having said that . . .

- **Don't count on drinking it right away.** Nothing is more tragic than gifting a bottle you're excited to try only to see it swept away and put into a closet. If you'd really like to drink what you bring, ask ahead about the evening's menu and find a wine you think is a good match (see page 106 for tips). When you arrive, tell the host: "This bottle is for you as a thank-you. I thought it would be perfect with the food tonight, so let me get it open."

- When in doubt, bring Champagne. It's a crowd-pleaser, good for any time of day, and every wine snob knows you can never have too much Champagne around, even if the "special occasion" you're toasting is a regular Tuesday night.

- Relax! No matter what you choose, you're doing something thoughtful for your host. If they trust your judgment, they'll be excited to try it, and if it's not a hit—hey, more for you! Regardless, they will be happy to receive a gift from you.

9 Handy Wine Tools

Most wine pros agree that fancy gadgets and doo-dads aren't necessary to enjoy wine—and some are a downright rip-off. With a good opener, a clean decanter, an all-purpose wineglass, and about 20 minutes to learn the ropes, you can handle almost any situation. Nevertheless, as a wine snob, you may want to have a few special tools on hand.

OPENERS

There are a few common tools for opening bottles of wine, each with different advantages. (For more on wine opening, check out page 83.)

- **Winged corkscrew:** The ubiquitous opener that looks a little like a stick-figure torso. As the name suggests, this tool's distinctive "wings" create the leverage to extract the cork.

- **Wine key (aka waiter's friend or waiter's tool):** The classic opener that fits snugly in your pocket or purse. This is the type of opener that somme-liers and professionals use. Mastering the tech-nique takes some practice (see instructions on page 84), but the convenience is well worth the effort—plus it gives you a great excuse to open more bottles of wine.

- **Ah so:** This double-pronged tool is useful for removing old corks, such as those in very old vintages. The prongs are inserted along the sides of the cork, rather than piercing the delicate center, which could cause the cork to break.

- **Durand:** A fancy and expensive trademarked two-part tool that combines the prongs of an ah so with the simple design of a waiter's friend. This tool is enjoying a great deal of popularity in the hipster wine crowd.

- **Rabbit:** A very common trademarked tool used by everyday consumers, this corkscrew is big but extremely user friendly. The corkscrew is inserted with the help of a simple lever; then by flipping the lever up in the opposite direction, the device removes the cork.

STORAGE TOOLS

If you'll be keeping a bottle around for a few days, you may need these items.

- **Decanters:** A wine snob staple, a decanter is a vessel into which wine is poured before being served. This serves a few purposes: One is to separate sediment that has fallen out of older red wines, so that you can enjoy a delicious old wine without a mouthful of unpleasant, sandlike grit. Another is to help wine breathe, opening up aromas and flavors. Young wines that need a little air open up faster in a decanter than in the bottle. Lastly, a decanter is a great accessory for bringing up the temperature of a cold wine. Keeping leftover wine in the fridge prolongs its freshness. Bring it back up to temperature quickly by transferring it to a decanter.

- Preservation gas: This product is used to fill the empty space of the wine consumed from an opened bottle to prevent the ingress of oxygen, which in turn delays the deterioration of the wine, so you don't have to finish that great bottle in one night. Typically a combination of nontoxic gases like argon, carbon dioxide, and nitrogen, preservation gas may be sold as "wine preserver" and can be found in wine shops and online. It is sold in canisters that come with a long straw; to use it, you spray the gas into the bottle using the straw, then immediately close the bottle with a stopper.

- **Stoppers or closures:** After you gas a wine (see above), you need a closure to seal it (rather than trying to shove the cork back in). Vacuum-style sealers are more effective than decorative stoppers; look for them online or at home-goods stores.

- **Alternative closures and packaging:** Bottles with screw caps are easy to reseal (not to mention easy to open), plus they eliminate the possibility of corked wine. Similarly, non-bottle packages are becoming more prevalent (and not just at college parties): wine snobs have a multitude of convenient (and unbreakable!) options like bag-in-box, juice boxes and pouches with straws, and mini plastic containers. As with bottled wines, some of these are good and some are decidedly sub-par. Bag-in-box and other non-bottled wines are also more economical (read: more wine for your buck), last longer without oxidizing, and are easier to ship, which means they have a smaller carbon footprint.

Stains, Souring, and Split Corks: Wine Troubleshooting

There's no use crying over spilled wine (unless it's a really excellent vintage). Not everything goes smoothly, so here's a handy guide to solving common wine-related snafus.

WINE STAINS

Nothing puts a damper on the evening like an accidental slosh of red onto a lovely white tablecloth. But fear not! First, blot up excess wine with paper towels, being careful not to rub it in. Next, cover the stained area with salt and let sit for a few minutes. Then stretch the stained fabric over a bowl and secure with a rubber band. Place the bowl in a sink and pour boiling water over the stain from a height of 6 to 8 inches (to give the water enough force to oust the stain). Launder as usual.

BROKEN CORKS

Even the pros sometimes break corks. If the cork breaks while still in the neck of the bottle, it's fine to dig back in with the corkscrew and try again. You may wind up with little particles of cork floating at the top of the wine, but those can be cleared out with a first small pour into a glass. If the cork is totally destroyed, pour the wine through a coffee filter or a piece of cheese cloth into a glass to catch all the little pieces.

GOOD WINE GONE BAD

A myriad of issues can negatively impact wine at any time from fermentation to bottling. The most common is corkiness, or the presence of a chlorine-based compound that gives the wine a musty, moldy, cardboard, or chlorine smell or taste. Other common issues are oxidation, which occurs when a cork has failed to seal, and plain old heat damage, if a wine has been stored in too warm an environment; both can result in an unwanted caramel, nutty, dried-fruit character. If you get a bottle of bad wine in a restaurant, send it back; if you bought it from your wine shop, ask about their policies on returning corked or damaged bottles.

HANGOVERS

Avoiding hangovers is easier said than done—even for the pros. First, and most obviously: don't drink so much! At tastings, limit your portions to small pours and don't be shy about spitting out a mouthful (see page 117). Also, drink one glass of water for every glass of wine to stay hydrated, and pad your stomach with some food to soak up the alcohol. If it's too late for prevention and you've woken up in agony, drink lots of water or herbal tea (peppermint and ginger will soothe your stomach) and eat some protein.

The Truth about Reviews and Ratings

You've probably noticed little signs on the shelves at the wine shop exclaiming 89 points this and 95 points that. What do these wine ratings mean, and who writes them?

In the United States, a few prominent wine-rating publications, including *Wine Spectator*, the *Wine Advocate*, *Wine & Spirits*, and *Wine Enthusiast*, provide ratings figures. These numbers often have a huge impact on what consumers buy and, therefore, a brand's popularity. The numbers ascribed to a wine by the writers of one publication can indicate a level of quality for a particular style or vintage, which helps consumers wade through the many wines on the market and help differentiate one from the next. However, the rubrics vary from publication to publication and are subjective—no one's running these wines through a tasting machine to extract a scientific truth.

In written reviews, the subjectivity is even more pronounced because the evaluation depends on the opinion of a single writer. Sure, a critic can provide some flowery prose about the flavors of the wine or assign a number to indicate relative quality. But no review or rating can tell you whether *you* will like the wine. A glowing review and a high score cannot guarantee that this wine is the right one for you. For a more personalized opinion, try ordering from a sommelier (see page 104) on your next restaurant visit.

How to Become a Sommelier

Who wouldn't want to taste, recommend, and buy wine for a living? If you'd like to take your love of wine to a professional level, here's the lowdown on the sommelier career.

The true definition of a sommelier is someone who holds the title of sommelier at a restaurant. Although it sounds like a very specific duty, the sommelier is an integral part of the restaurant's front-of-house team, doing everything from buying wine and other beverages and managing the cellar during the day to selling the wine on the restaurant floor at night.

Unlike Europe, the United States has few sommelier trade schools that are accredited by an independent educational body (though some schools offer classes and certificates). So most folks looking to work as a sommelier move up the ranks from other front-of-house positions or start out as an "intern," or junior sommelier, to learn from the head sommelier.

Other professional positions include working in sales at an importer or distributor, in retail at a wine shop, in wine education, or at a winery (to name a few). In all aspects of the business, there are many education opportunities and professional certifications, such as the following:

- **Court of Master Sommeliers:** Education and examinations geared toward sommeliers in restaurants.
  mastersommeliers.org

- **Wine and Spirit Education Trust:** A global wine and education body with exams and certifications in wine, spirits, and sake.
  wsetglobal.com

- **Society of Wine Educators:** Education, examinations, and conferences for those involved in the wine trade, from sommeliers and wine stewards to importers, distributors, hoteliers, and wine industry media professionals.
  societyofwineeducators.org

Wines of the World

Wine is one of the most popular beverages worldwide, and almost every country, culture, and continent has its own variety to offer. Here's a list of some top types to know and try.

EUROPE

The cradle of wine making, Europe is home to some revered and time-honored wines. In many European wine regions, the name of the region is often on the label, but many labels feature both region and grape variety, and a few mention variety alone.

ITALY

Named Entoria, meaning land of the vine, by the Greeks, Italy has a couple thousand indigenous grape varieties. You could spend a lifetime exploring, tasting, and enjoying the wines from each of the country's twenty unique regions (and if you can, you should!). Get started with these grapes, listed with their associated regions.

- Aglianico (Campania)

- Arneis (Piedmont)

- Corvina (Amarone, Veneto)

- Dolcetto (Piedmont)
- Fiano (Campania)
- Friulano (Friuli)
- Garganega (Soave, Veneto)
- Greco (Campania)
- Lagrein (Trentino-Alto Adige)
- Lambrusco (Emilia-Romagna)
- Moscato (Piedmont)
- Nerello Mascalese (Sicily)
- Nero d'Avola (Sicily)
- Teroldego (Trentino-Alto Adige)
- Verdicchio (Marche)

FRANCE

A country that, over thousands of years of viticulture, has practically become synonymous with wine. Aside from the famous varieties that we know and love, there are many other unique wines to seek out—some at an amazing value!

- Alicante Bouschet (Languedoc-Roussillon)
- Carignan (Languedoc-Roussillon)
- Chenin blanc (Loire Valley, especially Vouvray and Montlouis)

- Fer Servadou (southwest, especially Marcillac)
- Marsanne (Rhône Valley)
- Melon de Bourgogne (Loire Valley)
- Mourvèdre (Bandol, Provence)
- Müller-Thurgau (Alsace)
- Picpoul (Languedoc)
- Romorantin (Loire Valley)
- Roussanne (Rhône Valley)
- Sauvignon blanc/sémillon blend (Bordeaux)

SPAIN
There is much more to Spain than just tempranillo. Check out some of these delicious, lesser-known grapes and wines.

- Bobal (Utiel-Requena)
- Garnacha (Aragon)
- Godello (Galicia)
- Mencia (Bierzo)
- Palomino (various regions)
- Prieto picudo (Tierra de León)
- Txakoli (Basque Country)
- Verdejo (Rueda)
- Xarel-lo/macabeo/parallada blend (Catalonia)

GERMANY

Thankfully, German wines include the name of the grape variety on the label. Win! Riesling is a favorite, but many other varieties are worth checking out, though they may be a bit harder to find.

- Dornfelder
- Gelber Muskateller
- Gewürztraminer
- Grauburgunder (aka pinot gris)
- Kerner
- Lemberger
- Portugieser
- Scheurebe
- Spätburgunder (aka pinot noir)
- Weissburgunder (aka pinot blanc)

NORTH AMERICA

California, Washington, and Oregon produce 90 percent of the wine made in the United States, with classic varietals such as chardonnay, cabernet sauvignon, and pinot grigio reigning supreme. Still, there are some varietals that North American winemakers particularly favor.

- Chambourcin
- Concord
- Norton
- Petite sirah
- Symphony
- Syrah (never gets its due in California or Washington!)
- Vidal
- Zinfandel

SOUTH AMERICA

The wine industry in South America was shaped by the arrival of European grape varieties brought by immigrants in the 1800s. Differences in location and climate have made these wines a unique expression of the grape variety from those grown in the old world. They have taken on a life of their own and become the calling cards of their new country—often even surpassing the production, quality, and popularity of the original.

- Bonarda (Argentina)
- Carménère (Chile)
- Malbec (Argentina)
- Pais (Chile, Argentina)

- Tannat (Uruguay)
- Torrontés (Argentina)

AUSTRALIA AND NEW ZEALAND

Although foreigners may tend to lump these two countries—and their wines—together, in fact each has developed a unique culture around wine making (and a healthy rivalry, to boot).

AUSTRALIA

Australian wine is joked about as being bulk-production Shiraz or for having animals on the label (aka critter labels). In fact this country's wine industry is rich and offers many fine wines with distinctive expressions to explore.

- Cabernet sauvignon (Coonawarra)
- Old vines Shiraz (Barossa)
- Pinot noir (Victoria, Mornington Peninsula)
- Riesling (Clare Valley)
- Sémillon (Hunter Valley)
- Sémillon/sauvignon blanc (Western Australia)

NEW ZEALAND

Although New Zealand is considered a new world wine region, much of the country has a cool to moderate climate and is able to produce wines with the zingy tartness reminiscent of the old world and those with intense fruit character that recalls new world types. Look for the grape varieties below.

- Cabernet sauvignon (Hawkes Bay)
- Pinot noir (Central Otago)
- Riesling (Central Otago)
- Sauvignon blanc (Marlborough)
- Syrah (Hawkes Bay)

SOUTH AFRICA

The quality of wines from South Africa is continuously on the rise. Similar to New Zealand, the country's warmer climate produces wines that often have the earthy character of old world wines and the ripeness and fruit character of new world wines. Seek out these two signature grapes in particular:

- Chenin blanc
- Pinotage

10 World-Class Wine Travel Destinations

It's easier than ever to get excellent international wine into your home, but for the wine snob with wanderlust, here are ten top travel destinations where you can sip and see the sights.

BARCELONA, SPAIN

Barcelona is one of the best cities for culture, food, wine, and architecture—and it's just a 45-minute drive from one of the largest sparkling wine regions in the world! Cava is Spanish sparkling wine made in the same way as Champagne but at a fraction of the cost, and it is traditionally produced in Catalonia, the region in which Barcelona is located.

SANTA BARBARA, CALIFORNIA

Beaches, cycling, and wine tasting: that's Santa Barbara in a nutshell. Enjoy exploring the town, and then take day trips to visit the wine growing areas about an hour's drive away. Start with the town of Lompoc near the cool coast, where the focus is on chardonnay and pinot noir. Then move inland to the super-cute hamlet (and former Danish colony) of Solvang, where you'll find warmer temperatures and full, rich reds made from grenache, merlot, and cabernet sauvignon.

WILLAMETTE VALLEY, OREGON

Fly into Portland—where there's great coffee, tasty doughnuts, amazing restaurants, and the Willamette River to enjoy—and rent a car for the 40-mile drive to the Willamette Valley. This burgeoning wine region boasts more than 500 welcoming wineries in a gorgeous setting with a strong focus on the pinot noir grape, as well as pinot gris and chardonnay.

FINGER LAKES, NEW YORK

Just a four-hour drive from New York City (or an hour or so from Rochester and Syracuse) are 11,000 acres of vineyards growing riesling, pinot noir, merlot, and cabernet franc. This is a very large region to explore: each of the eleven lakes has a wine trail with great food and a bucolic waterside setting. All that plus apples, fall foliage, waterfalls, and the "gorges" college town of Ithaca.

MARLBOROUGH, NEW ZEALAND

Think of the scenery in *The Hobbit* or *The Lord of the Rings*, plus vines as far as the eye can see, and you've got Marlborough—no doubt one of the most striking views imaginable. Two-thirds of the plantings there are white grape varieties, the vast majority being sauvignon blanc; pinot noir is the dominant red grape. If you have time to island-hop, visit the North Island to explore the wines of Hawke's Bay, especially cabernet sauvignon and Syrah. (Fun fact: thanks to their location, New Zealand vineyards are the first on our planet to see the sun each day!)

MENDOZA, ARGENTINA

Mendoza is a short flight from Buenos Aires or Santiago, Chile. Here, in the dramatic foothills of the Andes Mountains, the red grape malbec is king.

CHAMPAGNE, FRANCE

Fly to Paris and enjoy a day in the City of Light, then head northeast by car or train 90 miles to Reims, in the heart of the famous region of Champagne. Taste all the sparkling wine your heart desires at one of the many open tasting rooms and take incredible cellar tours of the area's many famous Champagne houses.

PIEDMONT, ITALY

Absolutely one of the best wine regions on Earth, with top-notch red wines and insanely delicious food to match, just an hour and a half from Turin.

Shop and dine in the village of Alba after a day of winding your way up and down through the many hilltop towns offering stunning views of the vineyards. Hunt for white truffles in fall and enjoy that delicacy at dinner with either a delicious splurge (Barolo or Barbaresco made from the nebbiolo grape) or a superb value (Barbera or dolcetto).

RHEINGAU, GERMANY

Less than half an hour from Frankfurt, the villages and vineyards of the Rheingau dot the banks of the Rhine River. About an hour's drive from there is Koblenz, where you can visit riesling paradise as you journey down the Moselle River to visit some of the world's most stunning vineyard sites.

BURGUNDY, FRANCE

The town of Beaune and the city of Lyon are heaven for foodies and wine pros alike, home to not only several of the best restaurants in France but also vineyards that produce some of the priciest wine on the planet. Beaune's town center boasts beautiful churches, quaint shops, and a fifteenth-century charitable hospital museum as a centerpiece. The epic weekly farmers market features myriad local cheeses, meats, and other artisan products.

10 Wines Sommeliers Love

Ask a group of sommeliers one question and you might get five different opinions. But the one thing we do agree on is what to drink! In my experience, wine pros tend to love the same kinds of wines. (Things *can* get a little hairy when we try to decide what producer and what vintage—yes, we truly are geeks!) Here's a list of the top favorites I've seen.

- Champagne
- Riesling
- White Burgundy (specifically Chablis)
- Red Burgundy
- Northern Italian red wines (Barolo and Barbaresco)
- Rosé
- Bordeaux
- Aged cabernet from California
- Any obscure sparkling wine
- Beer (well, we can't drink wine all day!)

ACKNOWLEDGMENTS

I would like to give my deepest thanks first and foremost to Blair Thornburgh, my editor at Quirk Books, for her ideas, patience, and expertise helping me get thoughts to paper. A sincere thank-you to Jane Morley at Quirk for introducing us and recommending me! I am grateful for the love and support from James Tidwell MS, my sister Lauren Monosoff, and my brother Micah Monosoff. There are never enough ways to say thank you. Finally, thank you to Parker for keeping me company each day and taking me on lots of nice walks.